SPECTRUM®

Writing

Grade 1

Published by Spectrum®
an imprint of Carson-Dellosa Publishing LLC
Greensboro, NC

Spectrum® is an imprint of Carson-Dellosa Publishing.

Send all inquiries to:
Carson-Dellosa Publishing
P.O. Box 35665
Greensboro, NC 27425

Printed in the USA   ISBN 978-1-4838-1196-3
11-098187811

Table of Contents Grade 1

Chapter 1 Writing Basics

Chapter 2 Writing a Story

Table of Contents, continued

Chapter 3 Writing to Inform

Chapter 4 Writing an Opinion

Chapter 1

Lesson 1 Name Things

Everything has a name. Look at each picture. Then, write the name of what you see.

1. I see a _____.

2. I see a _____.

3. I see a _____.

Lesson 1 Name Things

_____

----

4. I see a _____.

_____

----

5. I see some _____.

_____

----

6. I see two _____.

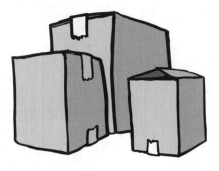

_____

----

7. I see many _____.

Lesson 2 Tell How You Feel

Words are used to tell how people feel. How do the people in these pictures feel? Write the word under each picture.

1. _____

2. _____

3. _____

4. _____

Lesson 2 Tell How You Feel

Complete each sentence to tell how each person feels.

I. This boy is _____

_____

_____

because _____.

2. This girl is _____

_____

_____

because _____.

Lesson 3 Tell How It Looks

Words are used to tell how things look.
How does the shell in this picture look?
We might use the words **bumpy** or **lumpy**.

Look at each picture. Answer the question.

1. Does this sheep look **hard** or **soft**?

_____

_ _ _ _ _ _ _ _ _ _ _ _ _ _ _ _ _

2. Does this flower look **blue** or **red**?

_____

_ _ _ _ _ _ _ _ _ _ _ _ _ _ _ _ _

3. Does this ring look **shiny** or **dull**?

_____

_ _ _ _ _ _ _ _ _ _ _ _ _ _ _ _ _

Lesson 3 Tell How It Looks

4. Is the duck **wet** or **dry**?

_____

- - - - - - - - - - - - - - - - -

_____

5. Is the pan **hot** or **cold**?

_____

- - - - - - - - - - - - - - - - -

_____

6. Is the boy **short** or **tall**?

_____

- - - - - - - - - - - - - - - - -

_____

7. Is the apple **red** or **green**?

_____

- - - - - - - - - - - - - - - - -

_____

Lesson 4 Describe It

Sometimes, more than one word is used to tell how something looks or feels. Trace the words.

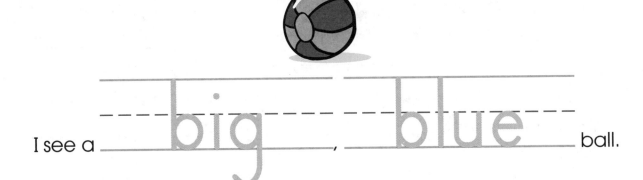

I see a ___big___ , ___blue___ ball.

Write the two words that tell how each thing looks.

warm
cold
snowy

_____ _____

1. It was a _____ , _____ day.

cute
tan
big

_____ _____

2. She is a _____ , _____ cat.

Lesson 4 Describe It

clean
messy
red

_____ _____

- -

3. Mike came in with _____, _____ shoes.

striped
blue
pink

_____ _____

- -

4. Here is my _____, _____ dress.

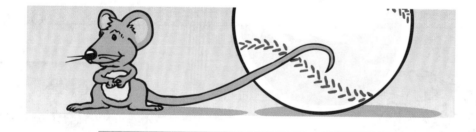

small
large
gray

_____ _____

- -

5. I see a _____, _____ mouse.

Lesson 4 Describe It

Read each question. Write your answers on the lines.

1. What words tell about a puppy?

_____   _____   _____

- - - - - - - - - - - -   - - - - - - - - - - - -   - - - - - - - - - - - -

_____   _____   _____

2. What words tell about a storm?

_____   _____   _____

- - - - - - - - - - - -   - - - - - - - - - - - -   - - - - - - - - - - - -

_____   _____   _____

3. What words tell about a birthday cake?

_____   _____   _____

- - - - - - - - - - - -   - - - - - - - - - - - -   - - - - - - - - - - - -

_____   _____   _____

4. What words tell about a winter coat?

_____   _____   _____

- - - - - - - - - - - -   - - - - - - - - - - - -   - - - - - - - - - - - -

_____   _____   _____

Lesson 5 What Is a Sentence?

A sentence is a group of words that tells a complete thought.

Here is a sentence about the girl in the picture below.

She is asleep.

Look at this sentence again.

She is asleep.

| A sentence always begins with a capital letter. | A sentence always ends with a period. |

Here are some more sentences. Circle the capital letter at the beginning of each sentence. Circle the period at the end.

1. The girl is waking up.

2. Her name is Pat.

3. Pat sits up in bed.

4. The sun is up.

5. Now, Pat is up, too.

Lesson 5 What Is a Sentence?

Here is a group of words.

She has over.

It has a capital letter at the beginning. It has a period at the end. But, it does not tell a complete thought. So, it is not a sentence.

Circle each group of words below that is a sentence.

She runs home.

Up the hill.

Calls to me.

I like to play.

Lesson 5 What Is a Sentence?

Sentences begin with a capital letter. They end with an end mark. This sentence is not correct.

we went to a movie

Here is how to correct it.

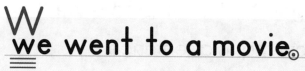

we went to a movie.

Now, correct these sentences. Use the same marks from above.

1. we were almost late.

2. it was dark in there

3. Sam fell asleep

4. everyone liked the movie

Questions to Ask About a Sentence
Does it begin with a capital letter? **Does it end with an end mark?** **Does it tell a complete thought?** **Is there space between each word?**

Lesson 6 Write a Sentence

Write the word that completes each sentence.

_____

– – – – – – – – – – – –

1. The _____ is up.

_____

– – – – – – – – – – – –

2. Tex likes his _____.

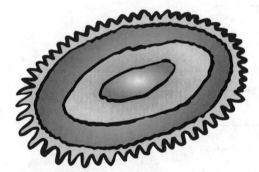

_____

– – – – – – – – – – – –

3. The _____ is on the floor.

Read each sentence again. Circle the capital letter. Circle the period.

Lesson 6 Write a Sentence

Remember: A sentence is a group of words that tells a complete thought. A sentence always begins with a capital letter and ends with a period.

Write a sentence about each picture. The first one is done for you.

The cup is blue.

1. _____

2. _____

Look at your sentences again. Did you leave a space between each word?

Lesson 6 Write a Sentence

3. _____

4. _____

5. _____

Now, read your sentences again. Does each sentence begin with a capital letter? Does each one end with a period? Correct any errors.

Lesson 7 Answer a Question

Answer each question. Write a complete sentence on the line.

The weather

today is

_____

_____

I. What color is your hair?

_____

_____

_____

_____

Lesson 7 Answer a Question

2. What part of the playground do you like best? Why?

_____

- -

_____

- -

_____

- -

_____

3. What is your favorite season? Why?

_____

- -

_____

- -

_____

- -

_____

Remember to check for complete sentences.

Questions to Ask About a Sentence

Does it begin with a capital letter?
Does it end with an end mark?
Does it tell a complete thought?
Is there space between each word?

Lesson 8 Ask a Question

Here is what you already know about a sentence:

- A sentence tells a complete thought.

- A sentence always begins with a capital letter.

- A sentence always ends with an end mark.

Another kind of sentence is called a **question**. A question asks something. Look at the question.

Is that a good book?

| A question always begins with a capital letter. | A question always ends with a question mark. |

Here are some more questions. Circle the capital letter that begins each sentence. Circle the question mark at the end.

1. May I read it?

2. Can Jim and Cal read it?

3. Is it about dogs?

4. Will you let me see?

5. Can we both see it?

Lesson 8 Ask a Question

Circle each question below.

1. I can read many books.

2. Can you read this one?

3. Will you read to me?

4. May I check these books out?

Lesson 8 Ask a Question

This sentence is not correct.

can we read this book

Here is how it is corrected.

C
can we read this book?

Now, correct these questions. Use the same marks from above.

1. Do you like this book

2. can we read another book?

3. have we read this one before

4. which one do you like best

Questions to Ask About a Question

Does it begin with a capital letter?
Does it end with a question mark?
Does it tell a complete thought?
Is there space between each word?

Chapter 1 Post-Test

What do you see? Write the words on the lines.

1. I see a _____.

2. The girl is _____

because _____.

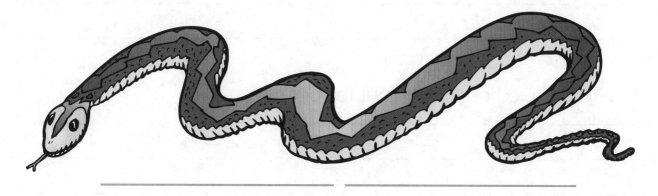

3. I see a _____, _____ snake.

Chapter 1 Post-Test

Write sentences.

_____

- - - - - - - - - - - - - - - - - - -

4. I like to _____

_____

- - - - - - - - - - - - - - - - - - -

because _____ .

5. Write a sentence. What is your favorite animal? Why?

_____

- - - - - - - - - - - - - - - - - - -

_____

_____

- - - - - - - - - - - - - - - - - - -

_____

6. Write a question to ask your teacher.

_____

- - - - - - - - - - - - - - - - - - -

_____

_____

- - - - - - - - - - - - - - - - - - -

_____

NAME _____

Look at the pictures. You can tell what happens first, next, and last. Label the pictures in order. Write **first**, **next**, and **last**.

_____ _____ _____

Lesson 1 Tell When

Look at the pictures. You can tell what happens first, next, and last.
Label the pictures in order. Write **first**, **next**, and **last**.

_____

- - - - - - - - - - - - - -

_____

_____

- - - - - - - - - - - - - -

_____

_____

- - - - - - - - - - - - - -

_____

_____

- - - - - - - - - - - - - -

_____

_____

- - - - - - - - - - - - - -

_____

_____

- - - - - - - - - - - - - -

_____

Lesson 2 What Is a Story?

A story always has a beginning, a middle, and an end.

These pictures tell a story. They show what happened at the beginning, in the middle, and at the end. Write **beginning**, **middle**, or **end** under the correct picture.

beginning

middle

end

Lesson 2 What Is a Story?

Look at these pictures. Write **beginning**, **middle**, or **end** under the correct picture.

_____

_____

_____

Now, write the story that these pictures tell. Write one sentence for the beginning of the story. Write one sentence for the middle of the story. Write one for the end of the story.

_____

_____

_____

_____

_____

_____

Lesson 2 What Is a Story?

Think of three things that happen in order. You might think about three things that you do at school each day. You might think about something you do with a pet or with a friend. Draw the three things that happen in order.

Now, tell your story. Tell what happens at the beginning, in the middle, and at the end. Make your story fun to read. Remember to leave a space between each word.

_____

_____

_____

_____

_____

_____

Lesson 3 Tell About a Place

A story happens at a place. You might tell what you see in a place. You might tell what you do in a place.

Anna wrote about a fun place. She wrote a complete sentence.

My room has lots of stuffed animals.

Write about your room. Remember to begin with a capital letter and end with a period.

_____

- -

_____

- -

_____

Now, write about a different place in your home.

_____

- -

_____

- -

_____

Lesson 3 Tell About a Place

Write about your favorite place. Where is it?

_____

– –

_____

– –

_____

Write a sentence that tells something you like to do in this place.

_____

– –

_____

_____

– –

_____

Ask a friend to read what you wrote and ask a question. Answer your friend's question below.

_____

– –

_____

_____

– –

Lesson 3 Tell About a Place

Ask an adult to help you use a book or the Internet to find a place you would like to go on vacation. Use the space below to list words about this place. Where is it located? What does it look like? Why do you want to go?

Lesson 3 Tell About a Place

Now, write two sentences about something that might happen in this place.

_____

- -

_____

- -

_____

- -

_____

- -

Read your sentences. Does each one begin with a capital letter? Does it end with an end mark? Imagine a story that could happen in this place. Tell your story to a friend.

Lesson 4 Tell What You Saw

It's fun to tell other people about the things we see. You can use sentences to help them "see" just what you saw.

Nick saw a butterfly yesterday. He wanted his friend to know just what it looked like. Here is what Nick wrote to his friend.

I saw a huge black butterfly. It had a little tail on each wing.

Can you "see" what the butterfly looked like? Draw a picture of it.

I. Imagine that the butterflies on this page are real. Write a sentence about them. Use words that really tell what the butterflies look like.

_____

— —

_____

_____

— —

_____

Lesson 4 Tell What You Saw

2. Imagine you saw this out of your window last night. Write a sentence about it.

_____

- - - - - - - - - - - - - - - - - - - -

_____

- - - - - - - - - - - - - - - - - - - -

_____

3. Ask an adult to help you use the Internet to find pictures of a big city in another country. Write a sentence about what you saw.

_____

- - - - - - - - - - - - - - - - - - - -

_____

- - - - - - - - - - - - - - - - - - - -

_____

Lesson 4 Tell What You Saw

4. Think about what you saw on the way to school this morning. Write a sentence about it. Help your reader "see" what you saw.

_____

- -

_____

- -

_____

5. Sometimes, you have to think hard to remember what you saw. Can you remember what a friend was wearing yesterday? Write a sentence that tells what one of your friends was wearing.

_____

- -

_____

- -

_____

- -

_____

Lesson 4 Tell What You Saw

6. Think about a time you saw something surprising, beautiful, or unusual. Write a sentence to describe what you saw.

_____

- -

_____

- -

_____

Now, ask a friend to read what you wrote on this page. Does your friend have a question about it? Write your sentence again. This time, change it to answer your friend's question.

_____

- -

_____

- -

_____

Now, look back at your sentences on pages 36–39. Do they begin with capital letters? Do they end with periods? Do they all have complete thoughts?

Lesson 5 Use Time-Order Words

Many events happen in a story. To help your reader follow your story, use words that tell the order in which things happen. Words that tell order include **before, then, after, suddenly,** and **finally**.

In the passage below, circle all the words that tell when something happened.

One day, Ava's parents told her she could get a new bike. Before she went to pick out the bike, Ava made sure she had all the things she needed to be safe when riding. First, she bought a helmet. Next, she bought kneepads. Finally, she bought elbow pads. After Ava had all the things she needed, she went to the bike store to choose her bike. Ava was very happy she had a new bike to ride.

Lesson 6 Write a Conclusion

The ending of a story is called the **conclusion**. A conclusion helps to tie a story together. In the story about Ava and her new bike on page 40, the conclusion tells the reader what happened after Ava bought her bike. Go back and read the story about Ava again. Underline the conclusion.

Now, write a different conclusion for the story.

Lesson 7 Write a Story

You will write a story about getting a new puppy. Get ready to write your story by thinking about things you might need to care for the puppy. Write a list of all the things you need below.

_____   _____

_____   _____

_____   _____

_____   _____

Now, think about what will happen in your story. Write a list of events in order.

_____

_____

_____

_____

_____

_____

Lesson 7 Write a Story

Now, write your own story. Use the ideas you wrote on page 42 to write a story about getting a puppy.

Use words such as **first**, **next**, **before**, **after**, **finally**, **suddenly**, and **last** to tell readers the order that events happen.

Write a good ending, or conclusion, for your story.

_____

- -

_____

- -

_____

- -

_____

- -

_____

- -

_____

Now, go back and read your story. Does each sentence begin with a capital letter and end with an end mark? Did you use words that tell the order of events? Does your story have a conclusion?

Lesson 8 Tell Today's Story

Look at what happened to Mary this morning.

Write the story of Mary's morning. Tell what happened at the beginning, in the middle, and at the end.

Mary's Crazy Day

_____

- -

_____

- -

_____

- -

_____

- -

_____

Lesson 8 Tell Today's Story

Have you ever had a crazy day? Draw three things that happened on your crazy day. Put them in order.

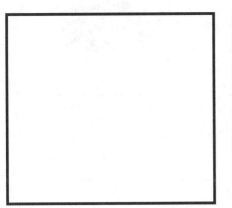  

Now, tell the story of your crazy day. Tell what happened at the beginning, in the middle, and at the end. Make your story fun to read.

_____

_ _

_____

_ _

_____

_ _

_____

_ _

_____

Lesson 9 Tell an Old Story

Do you remember a trip you took with your family?
It is fun to tell stories about things we remember.
Write about some things you remember from
the trip.

1. I remember _____

_____

_____

2. I remember _____

_____

_____

3. I remember _____

_____

_____

Lesson 9 Tell an Old Story

Now, ask an adult to help you find pictures, videos, or souvenirs from the trip you wrote about on page 46. After looking at these, do you remember more about the trip? Ask family members what they remember. Write new memories about the trip on the lines below.

Lesson 9 Tell an Old Story

Now, use the memories you gathered on pages 46 and 47 to write a story about a trip you took with your family. Make sure to use words that tell your reader the order in which the events happened.

_____

- -

_____

_____

- -

_____

_____

- -

_____

_____

- -

_____

Questions to Ask About a Story

Does it have a beginning, middle, and end?
Does each sentence begin with a capital letter?
Does each sentence end with an end mark?
Is there a space between each word?
Does every sentence belong?

Lesson 9 Tell an Old Story

Read the story you wrote on page 48 again. Does your story tell the order of events? Does it have a good ending, or conclusion? The conclusion might tell your reader if you enjoyed the trip or if you would like to go again.

Now, write your story again. Make it even better. Add a title. Then, ask yourself the questions on the bottom of page 48 again.

_____

_____

_____

_____

_____

_____

_____

_____

_____

_____

_____

Lesson 10 Tell a New Story

Some stories have people in them. Some stories have animals in them.
Plan a story that has animals in it. First, think about animals you might
like to use in your story. Write a list of animals.

_____   _____

_____   _____

_____   _____

_____   _____

Choose one animal for your story. Write some words that tell about the
animal. How does it look? How does it act?

_____

_____

My animal: _____

Describe your animal (for example, tell its size or color).

_____   _____

_____   _____

Write a sentence about something your animal might do.

_____

_____

Lesson 10 Tell a New Story

Now, think about what will happen at the beginning, in the middle, and at the end of your story. Write ideas for each part.

beginning

middle

end

Lesson 10 Tell a New Story

Now, write your story. Follow the plan you made on page 51. Remember to tell how things look and feel. Help your readers "see" what you write about.

_____

_____

_____

_____

_____

_____

_____

_____

_____

_____

Questions to Ask About a Story

Does it have a beginning, middle, and end?

Does each sentence begin with a capital letter?

Does each sentence end with an end mark?

Is there a space between each word?

Does every sentence belong?

Lesson 11 Stay on Topic

When you write a story, tell just one story at a time. Your story will be easier to understand.

Mike wrote a story. It is about his big sister. Read Mike's story.

Mel's New Bike

Mel has a new red bike. Mel and Mom put on their helmets. They rode their bikes around the block. They got hot and stopped for ice cream. My favorite kind of ice cream is vanilla. Mel loves her new bike.

Mike's story has a beginning, middle, and an end. Each sentence is written correctly. However, Mike wrote a sentence that doesn't belong in the story. The story is about Mel and her bike. Find the sentence that does not belong and write it below.

_____

- -

_____

- -

_____

- -

_____

Lesson 11 Stay on Topic

Tina wrote about her cat. Read Tina's story. Look for a sentence that does not belong.

Bob the Cat

Bob woke me up this morning. He licked my nose. That is how he always wakes me up. Bob is three years old. I push him away. Then he licks again. As soon as I get up, Bob curls up on my pillow. He is only looking for a warm spot to sleep.

Now, check Tina's story.

Find the beginning, middle, and end of the story. Write **b**, **m**, and **e** where each part starts.

Circle the capital letter that begins each sentence.

Put a box around the period that ends each sentence.

Draw a line through the sentence that does not belong.

Lesson 11 Stay on Topic

Can you stay on topic? Write a story about a bike, a pet, or something else that you like. Give your story a beginning, a middle, and an end. Make sure every sentence belongs.

_____

_____

_____

_____

_____

_____

_____

_____

_____

_____

_____

Now, check your story.

Questions to Ask About a Story

Does it have a beginning, middle, and end?
Does each sentence begin with a capital letter?
Does each sentence end with an end mark?
Is there a space between each word?
Does every sentence belong?

Chapter 2 Post-Test

1. Put the following words in order on the lines below: **last**, **next**, **first**, **then**.

_____   _____

- - - - - - - - - - - - -   - - - - - - - - - - - - -

_____   _____

- - - - - - - - - - - - -   - - - - - - - - - - - - -

_____   _____

2. Remember the last game that you played. Write a sentence about it.

_____

- -

_____

3. Remember your first day of school. What did you do to get ready to go to school? Write three things you did below.

_____

- -

_____

- -

_____

- -

_____

Chapter 2 Post-Test

4. Now, use the things you remembered about your first day of school to write a story below.

_____

- -

_____

- -

_____

- -

_____

- -

_____

5. Did you write a good ending to your story? Use this space to write a conclusion.

_____

- -

_____

- -

_____

Chapter 3

Lesson 1 What Is a How-to?

Have you ever put a toy together? Maybe you did an art project. Do you remember how you did it? You must have done things in order.

Matt did an art project. Here are the steps he followed.

Now, look at the steps.

How to Make a Sock Puppet

First, get a sock, yarn, buttons, and glue.

Next, glue on the yarn and buttons for hair and eyes.

Last, put your new sock puppet on your hand.

There are three steps in order.

The words **first**, **next**, and **last** make the order of the steps very clear.

Each step is a complete sentence.

Lesson 1 What Is a How-to?

When you tell how to do something, make sure you put the steps in order.

Jill wants to make a card for her grandmother. She has paper and crayons to make the card. Draw three steps in order that Jill needs to follow. Then, label your pictures **first**, **next**, and **last**.

 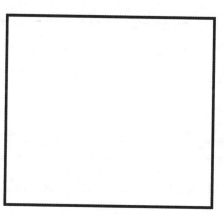 

Now, write about how to make a card. Give three steps. Use the words **first**, **next**, and **last** to show what order the steps are in.

Lesson 1 | What Is a How-to?

Now, ask a friend to read the directions you wrote on page 59. Ask your friend to tell if you are missing any steps. Rewrite your directions to include any steps you missed.

_____

- -

_____

- -

_____

- -

_____

- -

_____

Read your directions again. Did you remember to use words such as **first**, **then**, **next**, and **last**?

Lesson 2 Write a How-to

Lee is going to make a snack. He wrote the steps in a chart.

> First, get out a muffin and cheese.

↓

> Then, put the cheese on the muffin.

↓

> Last, have Mom heat the muffin in the oven until cheese melts.

You know how to do many things. You know how to make things and how to play games.

List some simple things you know how to do.

_____

_____

_____

_____

_____

_____

Lesson 2 Write a How-to

Choose one thing you listed on page 61. Think about how to do it. What are the steps? List them in this chart.

_____

— — — — — — — — — — — — — — — — — — — —

How to _____

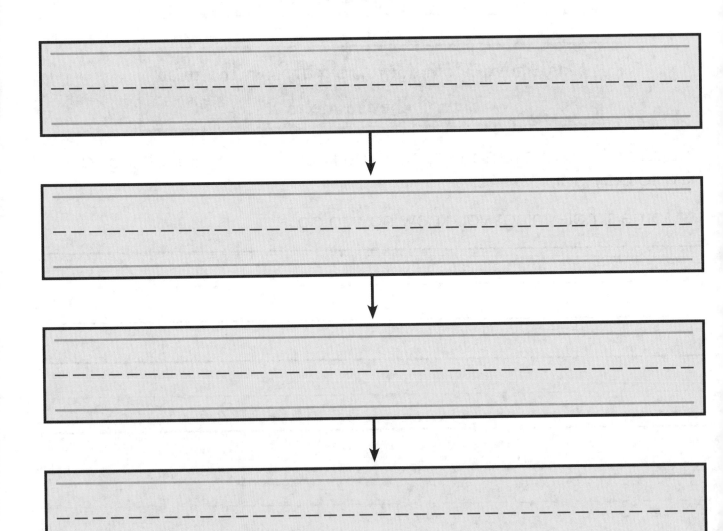

Lesson 2 Write a How-to

Now, write your steps. Use your chart on page 62 to keep the steps in order. Begin your sentences with **first**, **next**, **then**, and **last**.

_____

How to _____

_____

_____

_____

_____

_____

_____

_____

_____

Questions to Ask About Telling How

Are the steps in order?
Do the words first, next, and last make the order clear?
Is each sentence complete?
Does each sentence begin with a capital letter?
Does each sentence end with an end mark?
Does every sentence belong?

Lesson 3 Share Information

Every day at school, you do some of the same things. You enter the classroom. You take things out of your backpack. You hang your backpack up. You know just what to do every day.

Pretend a new classmate joins the class. She does not know anything about your classroom or what to do. Your teacher asks you to write down some of the steps. First, draw pictures to show what you do each day.

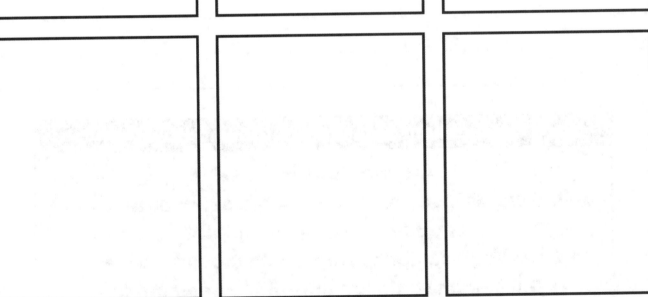

Lesson 3 Share Information

Look back at your pictures. Are the steps in order? If not, number them. Now, write the instructions for your new classmate. Use time-order words such as **first**, **next**, and **last**.

What to Do in Our Classroom

_____

- -

_____

- -

_____

- -

_____

- -

_____

- -

_____

Questions to Ask About Telling How

Are the steps in order?
Do the words first, next, and last make the order clear?
Is each sentence complete?
Does each sentence begin with a capital letter?
Does each sentence end with an end mark?
Does every sentence belong?

Lesson 3 Share Information

Now, look back at your writing. Is there anything you want to change? Could you add words to make something more clear? Does every sentence stay on topic? Ask an adult to read your instructions. Did you forget any steps?

Write your instructions again. Make them even better using what you learned from your adult reader. When you finish writing, ask yourself the questions on the bottom of page 65.

What to Do in Our Classroom

_____

_____

_____

_____

_____

_____

_____

_____

_____

_____

_____

Lesson 4 Tell What You Know

What do you want to **know how to do? List some** ideas.

_____   _____

_ _ _ _ _ _ _ _ _ _ _ _   _ _ _ _ _ _ _ _ _ _ _ _

_____   _____

_ _ _ _ _ _ _ _ _ _ _ _   _ _ _ _ _ _ _ _ _ _ _ _

_____   _____

Now, choose one **idea to write about.**

_____

_ _

_____

Ask an adult to help **you find three how-to books or** Web sites. Write
the steps you find on **the lines below.**

_____

_ _

_____

_____

_ _

_____

_____

_ _

_____

Lesson 4 Tell What You Know

Use what you have learned to write your own how-to. Try to make readers "see" what you are talking about.

_____

_ _

_____

_____

_ _

_____

_____

_ _

_____

_____

_ _

Questions to Ask About Your Writing

Does each sentence begin with a capital letter?
Does each sentence end with a period?
Is there a space between each word?
Do you tell what you know so that readers can "see" what you are talking about?
Does each sentence belong?

Lesson 5 Compare It

How are these trees the same? How are they different?

One tree is taller than the other. When we look at how things are the same and different, we compare them.

Compare these two pictures. Which one is larger? Which one is smaller? Then, complete each sentence.

The first house is _____.

The second house is _____.

Lesson 5 Compare It

What is the same about these balls? What is different? Complete the sentences.

_____

_ _ _ _ _ _ _ _ _ _ _ _ _ _ _ _ _ _ _

The balls are the **same** _____.

_____

_ _ _ _ _ _ _ _ _ _ _ _ _ _ _ _ _ _ _

The balls are **different** _____.

Compare this apple and orange. Write sentences to tell how they are the same and how they are different.

_____

_ _

_____

_ _

_____

_ _

_____

Lesson 5 Compare It

Ask an adult to help you use an online encyclopedia to find two different animals to compare. Answer the questions with complete sentences.

I will compare _____ and _____.

How are they the same?

_____

_____

_____

_____

How are they different?

_____

_____

_____

_____

Lesson 6 Write a Friendly Letter

A **friendly letter** is a letter you might write to someone you know. You might write to a friend, a sister, or a grandfather. You might write to tell the person what you have been doing. Or, you might write to cheer the other person up.

Josh wrote a letter to his grandmother. Why do you think Josh wrote this letter?

November 8

Dear Grandma,

How are you? Mom says you have a bad cold. I hope you don't feel too sick. Maybe some of your good soup would help.

My soccer team won its last game. We didn't win very many others, but I'm glad we won the last one. I will send you a picture of my team.

I hope you feel better soon.

Love,
Josh

Josh wrote this letter because _____

_____

_____

Lesson 6 Write a Friendly Letter

Look at Josh's letter.

There is a date at the top.

November 8

Dear Grandma,

This is the greeting. The word **Dear** always begins with a capital letter.

There is always a comma after the person's name.

How are you? Mom says you have a bad cold. I hope you don't feel too sick. Maybe some of your good soup would help.

My soccer team won its last game. We didn't win very many others, but I'm glad we won the last one. I will send you a picture of my team.

I hope you feel better soon.

This is the body of the letter.

This is the closing. The word may be different, but there is always a comma after the word.

Love,
Josh

The person writing the letter always signs his or her name.

Lesson 6 Write a Friendly Letter

Label the parts of Lora's letter.

_ _ _ _ _ _ _ _ _ _ _

_ _ _ _ _ _ _ _ _ _ _

_ _ _ _ _ _ _ _ _ _ _

February 9

→ Dear Kathy,

    Thanks for your letter. I liked reading about your trip to Idaho. Now I know where my potatoes come from.

    I am getting ready for spring break. I will write you a letter from my sunny backyard.

→   Your friend,
       Lora

Write a greeting for a friendly letter to a grandparent.

_ _ _ _ _ _ _ _ _ _ _ _ _ _ _ _ _ _

Write a closing for a friendly letter to a cousin or friend.

_ _ _ _ _ _ _ _ _ _ _ _ _ _ _ _ _ _

_ _ _ _ _ _ _ _ _ _ _

Lesson 6 Write a Friendly Letter

Pretend your class is learning about weather. You have many questions. You decide to ask someone who really knows about weather. Begin to plan a letter to Will the Weather Guy.

What kinds of weather could you ask about? List some here.

_____   _____

_____   _____

_____   _____

_____   _____

Ask an adult to help you use a newspaper or computer to check the weather forecast. What questions could you ask Will the Weather Guy about today's forecast?

_____

_____

_____

_____

Lesson 6 Write a Friendly Letter

Write a letter to Will the Weather Guy. Show the three parts of a friendly letter from page 73.

Lesson 6 Write a Friendly Letter

Look back at your letter. Did you include all three parts of a friendly letter? Are the questions in the body of your letter clear? Ask a friend to read your letter and give ideas for making it even better. Write your letter again. Send your letter as an e-mail to a real weather expert.

Lesson 7 Share Ideas

Imagine that something great has happened. Maybe the world's biggest tree house just landed in your backyard. Maybe your family just got back from sailing around the world. Whatever it is, you want to write and tell about it.

First, decide what the news is and who will want to know. Write to someone you know.

_____

I will write to _____ about

_____

_____.

Think about your news. Draw some things that you saw or some things that happened.

Lesson 7 Share Ideas

Look back at your pictures. List some words that describe your news.

_____ _____

_ _ _ _ _ _ _ _ _ _ _ _ _ _ _ _ _ _ _ _ _ _ _ _

_____ _____

_ _ _ _ _ _ _ _ _ _ _ _ _ _ _ _ _ _ _ _ _ _ _ _

_____ _____

Remember, your reader will want to "see" the news. What do things look like? What do they feel like?

Before you begin your letter, practice some parts of the letter.

Write your greeting. Remember to put a comma after the person's name.

_____

_ _

_____

Write your closing. Don't forget the comma.

_____

_ _

_____

Lesson 7 Share Ideas

Now, write your letter. Look back at your ideas on pages 78 and 79. Try to get the news in the correct order.

_____

- -

_____

- -

_____

- -

_____

- -

_____

- -

_____

Questions to Ask About a Friendly Letter

Does your greeting begin with Dear?
Is there a comma after the person's name in the greeting?
Is there a comma after your closing?
Did you sign your name?

Lesson 7 Share Ideas

Look at your letter again. Find the three parts of a friendly letter. Are they all there? Ask a friend to read your letter. Can your friend "see" your news? Ask him or her for ideas to make the letter better. Write your letter again. Send your letter in the mail or type it on a computer and send it as an e-mail.

Lesson 8 Write a Note

Notes are used in many ways. Write a note to a friend. Write about what you did last weekend.

_____

- - - - - - - - - - - - - - - -

_____

_____

- -

_____

_____

- -

_____

_____

- -

_____

_____

- -

_____

_____

- - - - - - - - - - - - - - - -

_____

Lesson 8 Write a Note

Now, write a note to a parent or an older brother or sister. Remember a time that he or she helped you. Tell why you are thankful for your parent, brother, or sister.

Chapter 3 Post-Test

Think of a reason to write a letter to someone you know. You might want to tell something. You might want to ask something. Remember to use the three parts of a friendly letter.

Chapter 3 Post-Test

Write a how-to. Imagine you have a class pet. His name is Harry the Hamster. Write directions for the class about how to take care of Harry. Use words such as **first**, **then**, **next**, and **last** in your directions.

_____

- -

_____

- -

_____

_____

- -

_____

_____

- -

_____

_____

- -

_____

_____

- -

_____

Chapter 4

Lesson 1 What Is an Opinion?

An **opinion** tells what you think about something. Your opinion can tell that you like or dislike something such as a book or movie. Your opinion can tell that you thought something was funny, silly, exciting, or scary. When you give an opinion, you should tell the reader why.

Last week, Caleb read a book about kangaroos. He liked the book so much that he wants his friend to read the book, too. In the following passage, Caleb gives his opinion about the book. Underline Caleb's opinions and circle the reasons for his opinions.

> Last week, I read a book about kangaroos. I liked it a lot. It was very exciting. First, I learned about where kangaroos live. They live in Australia. Then, I learned that kangaroos carry their babies in pouches on the front of their bodies. This was very funny! Next, I learned that kangaroos like to eat grass and fruit. Finally, I learned that kangaroos can jump ten feet high. I learned a lot about kangaroos in this book. I think you should read it, too.

Lesson 1 What Is an Opinion?

Read the sentences below. Underline each fact. Circle each opinion.

Green beans are vegetables.

That game is fun to play.

I should be allowed to stay up later.

It rained two times last week.

Broccoli is the best vegetable.

She wore a pretty dress.

Now, practice writing an opinion. Think of a book you read. Write the title to complete only one of the sentences below. This sentence tells your opinion.

_____

I enjoyed reading _____.

_____

I did not enjoy reading _____.

Lesson 2 Write Reasons

Think about asking your teacher or your parent for something special, like an extra recess or dessert. Would you give reasons why you think you deserve the treat? Of course you would!

It is the same when you write an opinion. You must give good reasons why you think your opinion is true. Imagine you are writing a note to your parent asking for a later bedtime. Circle good reasons for your opinion.

I am sleepy.

I want to finish reading a good book.

I do not have school in the morning.

I am not sleepy yet.

You let me stay up late last night.

I have to get up early in the morning.

Now, think about the book you wrote about on page 87. Why did you like it or not like it? Maybe you thought the story was exciting or dull. Maybe you liked the pictures or did not like the ending. It is up to you! Below, list three reasons for your opinion.

_____

_____

_____

_____

_____

_____

Lesson 3 Select a Topic

When you write to share an opinion, it is a good idea to choose a topic that makes different people have different feelings. For example, some students like math better and some students like art class better. Some people think a sport is fun to play, while others find it boring.

Think about topics that make people feel different ways. List them below.

_____   _____

_____   _____

_____   _____

Choose one topic that you have strong feelings about. Write it below.

_____

Lesson 4 Write an Opinion

Look at the topic you chose on page 89. Complete the sentence below to write your opinion about the topic.

_____

‒ ‒

I feel that _____

_____

‒ ‒

_____.

Now, think of three reasons for your opinion. Write them below.

_____

‒ ‒

_____

‒ ‒

_____

_____

‒ ‒

_____

Lesson 4 Write an Opinion

Write a letter to a friend explaining the opinion you wrote on page 90. Use the ideas you wrote on page 90. Give the topic. State your opinion. Give good reasons why you feel the way you do. Finally, write a conclusion that gives a good ending to your letter.

Lesson 4 Write an Opinion

Read the opinion letter you wrote on page 91. Ask yourself the questions at the bottom of this page.

Ask a friend to read your letter and answer the questions, too. Does your friend feel the same way about the topic that you do? If not, ask your friend for ideas to make the letter stronger.

Now, rewrite your opinion letter to make it even better.

_____

_____

_____

_____

_____

_____

_____

_____

_____

Questions to Ask About an Opinion
Did you give your opinion?
Did you tell the reader why?
Did you include a conclusion?

Lesson 5 Why I Should Have a Pet

Choose an animal you would like to have as a pet. Now, write three reasons why you should be able to have this pet.

_____

_ _ _ _ _ _ _ _ _ _ _ _ _ _

I want to have _____ as a pet.

_____

_ _ _ _ _ _ _ _ _ _ _ _ _ _

I should be able to have _____ as a pet because:

_____

_ _

_____

_ _

_____

_ _

_____

Lesson 5 Why I Should Have a Pet

Now, ask an adult to help you use a book or the Internet to find out what this pet needs. How big should the cage be? What does it like to eat? How often does it need to be fed? Does it need to live inside or outside? Write about what your pet needs on the lines below.

Lesson 5 Why I Should Have a Pet

Use the ideas you wrote on pages 93 and 94 to write about why you should have the pet you want. Remember to tell your opinion. Give good reasons to support your opinion. Use facts you learned to make your writing stronger. Write a conclusion at the end.

Lesson 5 Why I Should Have a Pet

_____

- -

_____

- -

_____

_____

- -

_____

_____

- -

_____

Go back and read what you wrote.

Questions to Ask About an Opinion
Did you give your opinion?
Did you give good reasons for your opinion?
Did you include facts?
Did you remember to write a conclusion?

Share your writing with a parent or teacher. Does he or she agree with your opinion?

Chapter 4 Post-Test

1. Write an opinion you have. It can be about a book, movie, or game.

_____

_ _

_____

_ _

_____

_ _

_____

2. Now, write two reasons why you have this opinion.

_____

_ _

_____

_ _

_____

_ _

Chapter 4 Post-Test

3. Write a letter to your friend about your favorite toy. Why do you like this toy? Do you think your friend should also get this toy?

_____

- -

_____

_____

- -

_____

_____

_____

- -

_____

_____

- -

_____

_____

- -

_____

Writer's Handbook

When should I use a capital letter?

The first word of a sentence always begins with a capital letter.
>   **T**he kitten jumped into my lap.

The word **I** is always spelled with a capital letter.
>   Kristen and **I** laughed at the kitten.

The name of a person or an animal always begins with a capital letter.
>   The kitten belongs to **K**risten.
>   The kitten's name is **M**eep.

Other kinds of names also begin with capital letters. Here are some examples:
>   streets: **M**artin **A**venue   **J**effers **R**oad
>   schools: **J**ackson **E**lementary **S**chool
>   towns and cities: **M**edford   **R**ome
>   states: **W**isconsin   **G**eorgia
>   countries: **C**anada   **I**taly
>   holidays: **L**abor **D**ay
>   days and months: **T**uesday   **J**uly
>   clubs and groups: **C**ub **S**couts   **V**alley **G**arden **C**lub
>   companies: **D**oggie **D**ay **C**are   **F**oster **P**aint **C**ompany

What are the rules about sentences?

A sentence must always tell a complete thought.
>   Complete thought: She meowed.
>   Complete thought: The kitten yawned and rolled over.
>   Not a complete thought: She again.
>   Not a complete thought: Around and around her.

Writer's Handbook

A sentence always begins with a capital letter.
>**C**arry the kitten carefully.

A sentence always ends with an end mark. There are three kinds of end marks. A sentence that tells something ends with a period.
>The kitten is soft**.**

A sentence that asks something ends with a question mark.
>Is the kitten soft**?**

A sentence that shows excitement or fear ends with an exclamation point.
>The kitten scratched me**!**

What is the writing process?

Writers use five steps when they write. These steps make up the writing process.

Step 1: Prewrite

First, writers think up ideas. This is called **prewriting**. They might write their ideas in a list. They might even make a chart and put their ideas in order.

Sam will write about his trip to the zoo. He put his ideas in a web.

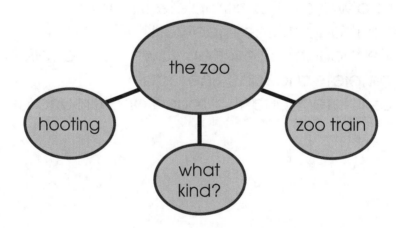

Writer's Handbook

Step 2: Draft

Next, writers put their ideas on paper. This is called a **first draft**. Writers know that there might be mistakes. That's okay. Most writers do not get everything perfect on the first try.

Here is Sam's first draft.

Zoo Noises

Every time I go, I learn something new. I went to the zoo three times last year. last week, I learned that there are many noises at the zoo. There was a funny hooting sound. I asked what kind that was Then, my brother told me it was the train whistle. I felt pretty silly. I wonder what I will learn next time I go to the zoo.

Step 3: Revise

Then, writers change or fix their first draft. This is called **revising**. They might move ideas around or add information. They might take out words or sentences that don't belong. Here are the changes that Sam made.

Zoo Noises

Every time I go ^(to the zoo), I learn something new. ~~I went to the zoo three times last year.~~ last week, I learned that there are many noises at the zoo. There was a funny hooting sound. I asked what kind ^(of animal) that was Then, my brother told me it was the train whistle. I felt pretty silly. I wonder what I will learn next time I go to the zoo.

Writer's Handbook

Step 4: Proofread

Writers usually write a new copy so their writing is neat. Then, they look again to make sure everything is correct. They look for mistakes in their sentences. This is called **proofreading**.

Sam wrote a new copy. Then, he found two last mistakes.

Zoo Noises

Every time I go to the zoo, I learn something new. <u>l</u>ast week, I learned that there are many strange noises at the zoo. I heard a funny hooting sound. I asked what kind of animal that was. Then, my brother told me it was the train whistle. I felt pretty silly. I wonder what I will learn next time I go to the zoo.

Step 5: Publish

Finally, writers make a final copy that has no mistakes. They are now ready to share their writing with a reader. They might choose to read their writing out loud. They can add pictures and create a book. There are many ways for writers to **publish**, or share, their work with readers.

Here is the final copy of Sam's writing about the zoo.

Zoo Noises

Every time I go to the zoo, I learn something new. Last week, I learned that there are many strange noises at the zoo. I heard a funny hooting sound. I asked what kind of animal that was. Then, my brother told me it was the train whistle. I felt pretty silly. I wonder what I will learn next time I go to the zoo.

Writer's Handbook

What different kinds of writing are there?

Writers sometimes write about things they have done or seen. They might tell about something funny, sad, or unusual. When Sam wrote about what he saw at the zoo, he was writing about real things that he did and saw.

Look at Sam's zoo story again.

The word **I** shows that the writer was part of the action.		A time-order word shows the order of events.

Zoo Noises

Every time I go to the zoo, I learn something new. Last week, I learned that there are many strange noises at the zoo. I heard a funny hooting sound. I asked what kind of animal that was. Then, my brother told me it was the train whistle. I felt pretty silly. I wonder what I will learn next time I go to the zoo.

Describing words help readers "see" or "hear" what is happening.

The writer stayed on topic. All of the sentences give more information about a zoo noise.

Writers sometimes write about made-up things. They might write about people or animals. The people and animals might seem real, but the writers made them up. Here is a made-up story that Shawn wrote.

Time-order words help keep ideas in order.

Describing words help readers "see" what is happening.

Shawn's Zoo

Shawn wants to be a zookeeper. Right now, he keeps small animals. He pretends that his mice and his cat are zoo animals.

Some day, he will keep big animals. He watches his gray mice running on their little wheel. At his zoo, Shawn will teach elephants to run on a big wheel. His cat chases a ball. At Shawn's zoo, the lions will play soccer against the tigers.

Shawn has lots of ideas for his zoo. He thinks his zoo will be a great zoo.

Shawn's readers will have fun reading his ideas.

The writer stayed on topic. All of the sentences give more information about a made-up zoo.

Writer's Handbook

Writers sometimes write about how to do things. They might tell how to play a game or make a snack. Sam has a favorite snack. He wrote about how to make it.

> The steps are all in order, starting with the items needed to make the snack.

> Order words help readers keep the steps in order.

Cracker-Cheese Surprise

First, set out wheat crackers, sliced olives, sliced cheese, and a metal pie plate. Lay out some crackers in the pie plate. Then, place one olive slice on each cracker. Place one slice of cheese on top of each cracker. Finally, ask a grown-up to set the pie plate under a broiler. Heat just until the cheese bubbles. Have the grown-up remove plate from broiler and let cool for several minutes. At last, you get to enjoy your healthy snack.

> Clear words help readers understand what to do.

Writers sometimes write to describe things. They might tell about an object, a place, or an event. They use good sense, or describing, words so that readers can see, hear, smell, feel, or taste whatever is being described. Read how Sam described his snack.

> **Sizzle** helps readers hear what is happening.

> **Warm** helps readers know how the snack feels.

I can tell when my snack is done because I hear a little sizzle from the oven. When my mom opens the broiler door, the cheese is bubbly. I can hardly wait for the crackers to cool. When I take a bite, the cracker crunches and the warm cheese stretches out in a long string like taffy. And then, that salty little olive slice is just waiting to surprise me. Yum!

> **Bubbly** helps readers see what is happening.

> **Salty** helps readers taste the snack.

Writer's Handbook

Writers write friendly letters to share news or ideas. They also write letters to get information. A friendly letter has four parts: the date, the greeting, the body, and the closing. Here is a letter Sam wrote to a friend about something that happened at the zoo.

Words in the greeting each begin with a capital letter.

There is always a comma after the person's name.

The date is in the upper, right corner.

August 26

Dear Kyle,

    Last week, while you were at camp, we went to the zoo. We had a great time.

    The best part was the elephants. Did you know that elephants love to take baths? The elephant keeper was spraying a hose at the elephants. The water shot up in a big spout. The elephants stood under the water just as if they were taking a shower. Then, one of them started to dance. Before long, all three of them were dancing in the shower!

    It's only a week until school starts. I'll show you my dancing elephant pictures on the first day of school.

        Your friend,
        Sam

The body of the letter gives information.

Only the first word of the closing begins with a capital letter. There is always a comma after the closing.

The writer signs his or her name.

Answer Key

Chapter I

Lesson I

Page 5
I see a pig.
I see a shoe.
I see a ball.

Page 6
I see a pen.
I see some fish.
I see two trucks.
I see many boxes.

Lesson 2

Page 7
happy
sad
mad
scared

Page 8
sleepy
Answers will vary.
excited
Answers will vary.

Lesson 3

Page 9
soft
blue
shiny

Page 10
wet
hot
tall
green

Lesson 4

Page 11
cold, snowy
cute, tan

Page 12
messy, red
pink, striped
small, gray

Page 13
Answers will vary.

Lesson 5

Page 14
The girl is waking up.
Her name is Pat.
Pat sits up in bed.
The sun is up.
Now, Pat is up, too.

Page 15
Circled sentences:
She runs home.
I like to play.

Page 16
We were almost late.
It was dark in there.

Sam fell asleep.
Everyone liked the movie.

Lesson 6

Page 17
(T)he sun is up₀
(T)ex likes his hat₀
(T)he rug is on the floor₀

Page 18
Answers will vary.

Page 19
Answers will vary.

Lesson 7

Page 20
Answers will vary.

Page 21
Answers will vary.

Lesson 8

Page 22
(May I read it?)
(Can Jim and Cal read it?)
(Is it about dogs?)
(Will you let me see?)
(Can we both see it?)

Page 23
Circled questions:
Can you read this one?
Will you read to me?
May I check these books out?

Page 24
Do you like this book?
Can we read another book?
Have we read this one before?
Which one do you like best?

Post-Test

Page 25
hat
Answers will vary.
Answers will vary.

Page 26
Answers will vary.

Chapter 2

Lesson 1

Page 27
last, next, first

Page 28
first, last, next
next, first, last

Lesson 2

Page 29
middle
beginning
end

Page 30
beginning
middle
end

Answer Key

Answers will vary.

Page 31
Pictures will vary.
Answers will vary.

Lesson 3

Page 32
Answers will vary.

Page 33
Answers will vary.
Answers will vary.
Answers will vary.

Page 34
Answers will vary.

Page 35
Answers will vary.
Answers will vary.

Lesson 4

Page 36
Students should draw a picture of a butterfly.
Answers will vary.

Page 37
Answers will vary.
Answers will vary.

Page 38
Answers will vary.
Answers will vary.

Page 39
Answers will vary.
Answers will vary.

Lesson 5

Page 40
Circle:
Before, First, Next, Finally, After

Lesson 6

Page 41
Underline:
Ava was very happy she had a new bike to ride.
Conclusions will vary.

Lesson 7

Page 42
Answers will vary.

Page 43
Answers will vary.

Lesson 8

Page 44
Answers will vary.

Page 45
Pictures will vary.
Answers will vary.

Answer Key

Lesson 9

Page 46
Answers will vary.

Page 47
Answers will vary.

Page 48
Answers will vary.

Page 49
Answers will vary.

Lesson 10

Page 50
Answers will vary.
Answers will vary.
Answers will vary.
Answers will vary.

Page 51
Answers will vary.

Page 52
Answers will vary.

Lesson 11

Page 53
My favorite kind of ice cream is vanilla.

Page 54
(b) Bob woke me up this morning. He licked my nose. That is how he always wakes me up. Bob is three

years old. **(m)** I push him away. Then he licks again. **(e)** As soon as I get up, Bob curls up on my pillow. He is only looking for a warm spot to sleep.

Page 55
Answers will vary.

Post-Test

Page 56
first, then, next, last OR first, next, then, last
Answers will vary.
Answers will vary.

Page 57
Answers will vary.
Answers will vary.

Chapter 3

Lesson 1

Page 59
Pictures will vary.
Answers will vary.

Page 60
Answers will vary.

Lesson 2

Page 61
Answers will vary.

Answer Key

Page 62
Answers will vary.

Page 63
Answers will vary.

Lesson 3

Page 64
Pictures will vary.

Page 65
Answers will vary.

Page 66
Answers will vary.

Lesson 4

Page 67
Answers will vary.
Answers will vary.
Answers will vary.

Page 68
Answers will vary.

Lesson 5

Page 69
The first house is larger.
The second house is smaller.

Page 70
size
colors
Answers will vary.

Page 71
Answers will vary.
Answers will vary.
Answers will vary.

Lesson 6

Page 72
Josh wrote this letter to tell
Grandma about his soccer game.

Page 74
greeting
body
closing
Answers will vary.

Page 75
Answers will vary.
Answers will vary.

Page 76
Answers will vary.

Page 77
Answers will vary.

Lesson 7

Page 78
Answers will vary.
Pictures will vary.

Page 79
Answers will vary.

Page 80
Letters will vary.

Answer Key

Page 81
Letters will vary.

Lesson 8

Page 82
Notes will vary.

Page 83
Notes will vary.

Post-Test

Page 84
Answers will vary.

Page 85
Answers will vary.

Chapter 4

Lesson 1

Page 86
Underline:
I liked it a lot. It was very exciting. This was very funny! I think you should read it, too.

Circle:
First, I learned about where kangaroos live. Then, I learned that kangaroos carry their babies in pouches on the front of their bodies. Next, I learned that kangaroos like to eat grass and fruit. Finally, I learned that kangaroos can jump ten feet high.

Page 87
Underline:
Green beans are vegetables. It rained two times last week.

Circle:
That game is fun to play. I should be allowed to stay up later. Broccoli is the best vegetable. She wore a pretty dress.

Responses will vary.

Lesson 2

Page 88
Circle:
I do not have school in the morning. I am not sleepy yet. I want to finish reading a good book.

Responses will vary.

Lesson 3

Page 89
Topics will vary.

Lesson 4

Page 90
Responses will vary.

Page 91
Letters will vary.

Answer Key

Page 92
Letters will vary.

Lesson 5

Page 93
Responses will vary.

Page 94
Responses will vary.

Page 95
Responses will vary.

Page 96
Responses will vary.

Post-Test

Page 97
Responses will vary.

Page 98
Responses will vary.